The Sarbanes-Oxley Act of 2002: Impacting the Accounting Profession

The Sarbanes-Oxley Act of 2002: Impacting the Accounting Profession

Mark S. Beasley • Randal J. Elder

PEARSON
Prentice Hall

Upper Saddle River, New Jersey 07458

VP/Editorial Director: Jeff Shelstad
Acquisitions Editor: Bill Larkin
Assistant Editor: Sam Goffinet
Manager, Print Production: Christy Mahon
Production Editor & Buyer: Carol O'Rourke
Printer/Binder: Courier, Bookmart Press

PEARSON
Prentice
Hall

10 9 8 7 6 5 4 3 2
ISBN 0-13-185526-3

TABLE OF CONTENTS

The Sarbanes–Oxley Act of 2002: Impacting the Accounting Profession

Mark S. Beasley
North Carolina State University

Randal J. Elder
Syracuse University

Pearson Prentice Hall, Inc.

INTRODUCTION

The Sarbanes–Oxley Act (the Act) was signed into legislation on July 30, 2002. Called by many the most significant securities legislation since the 1933 and 1934 Securities Acts, the provisions of the Act apply to publicly held companies and their audit firms. The Act was triggered by the December 2001 bankruptcy of Enron just over a month after it admitted accounting errors that inflated earnings since 1994 by almost $600 million. With $62 billion in assets, it was the largest bankruptcy case in U.S. history. It was dwarfed several months later by the massive fraud and bankruptcy filing of WorldCom in July 2002, with $100 billion in assets. Enron and WorldCom were both audited by Andersen, a Big 5 audit firm. Andersen essentially ceased to exist after the firm was found guilty of obstruction of justice in the Enron case in June 2002. Reported instances of fraud and alleged audit failure at several other high-profile companies suggest that concerns about auditor performance were not limited to Andersen.

A key provision of the Sarbanes–Oxley Act is the creation of the Public Company Accounting Oversight Board (the PCAOB). With the creation of the PCAOB, the accounting profession, which had been largely self-regulated, is now a regulated profession for the audits of public companies. The PCAOB provides oversight for auditors of public companies, including establishing auditing, ethics, independence, and quality control standards for public company audits, and performing inspections of the quality controls at audit firms under its oversight.

An important issue in the Enron case was the large amount of fees paid to Andersen for non-audit services. Andersen Consulting was the first consulting practice to separate from a Big 5 accounting firm, and three of the remaining Big 4 firms have since disposed of their consulting practices. The Act restricts the ability of auditors to provide non-audit services to their public company audit clients and allows the PCAOB to establish other provisions affecting auditor independence.

Enron, WorldCom and other high-profile examples of fraudulent financial reporting highlighted weaknesses in corporate governance. The Act includes provisions to improve the independence and effectiveness of audit committees. The Act also requires the CEO and CFO to certify the company's financial statements, with harsh penalties for willful certification of financial statements that are known to be materially misstated.

Perhaps the most significant provision of the Act is the requirement in Section 404 that management report its assessment of the effectiveness of internal control over financial reporting. The auditor must attest to these management reports on the effectiveness of internal controls. PCAOB Auditing Standard No. 2 provides guidance for audits of the effectiveness of internal control.

Cases of fraud at companies like Enron and WorldCom illustrate the need for additional guidance for auditors in detecting fraud. SAS No. 99 was issued by the Auditing Standards Board in 2002 to provide additional guidance to auditors in identifying and responding to the risk of fraud. This standard also provides useful insights to all key corporate governance players who together work to prevent, deter, and detect financial reporting fraud.

Significant provisions of the Sarbanes–Oxley Act and related changes in the accounting profession are described in the following pages. This is followed by discussion of the fraud guidance in SAS No. 99. A summary of the key provisions and organizational structure of the Act is included in the Appendix.

CHANGES IN THE REGULATORY ENVIRONMENT

Establishment of Public Company Accounting Oversight Board (PCAOB)

The Sarbanes–Oxley Act dramatically changes oversight of the accounting profession by establishing the Public Company Accounting Oversight Board, which is appointed and overseen by the SEC. The Board is made up of five full-time members and oversees and investigates the audits and auditors of public companies. As required by Sarbanes–Oxley, the SEC announced on April 24, 2003 that the PCAOB was appropriately organized and able to carry out the requirements of the Sarbanes–Oxley Act.

- *Board composition* - Two of the five Board members must be or must have been CPAs. The remaining three must not be and cannot have been CPAs. The Chair may be held by one of the CPA members, but he or she must not have practiced accounting during the five years preceding his/her appointment.
- *Funding* – The PCAOB is funded by mandatory fees on public companies. Accounting firms that audit public companies must register with the PCAOB ("registered firm") and pay registration and annual fees.
- *Standard setting* – The Board will issue or adopt standards set by other groups for audit firm quality controls for the audits of public companies. These standards include auditing and related attestation standards, quality control, ethics, independence, and "other standards necessary to protect the public interest."
- *Investigative and disciplinary authority* – The Board can regularly inspect registered accounting firms' operations and will investigate potential violations of securities laws, standards, competency, and conduct.

Appointment of PCAOB Chair – Appointment of a chairman of the PCAOB proved to be controversial. Former CIA and FBI chief William Webster was appointed chairman in October 2002 in a contested vote, but resigned three weeks later due to controversy involving his role as head of the audit committee of a company involved in questionable accounting. William McDonough, former head of the New York branch of the Federal Reserve, was subsequently appointed chairman in April 2003.

Auditing Standards

Section 103 of the Sarbanes–Oxley Act provides that the PCAOB shall establish auditing, quality control, and ethics standards to be followed by registered CPA firms in their audits of public companies. The Act allowed the PCAOB to designate or recognize a professional group of accountants to propose new standards. However, in April 2003 the PCAOB announced that they would not delegate this authority, and would assume responsibility for establishing auditing standards. The PCAOB adopted existing auditing standards as of April 16, 2003 issued by the AICPA's Auditing Standards Board (ASB) as the PCAOB's Interim Auditing Standards.

Since April 2003, the PCAOB has issued three standards. PCAOB Auditing Standard No. 1 requires auditors of public companies to refer to auditing and related professional practice standards established by the PCAOB in audit reports for public companies.

Standard No. 2 addresses audits of internal control performed in conjunction with an audit of financial statements as required by Section 404 of the Sarbanes–Oxley Act. PCAOB Standard No. 3, issued largely in response to the alleged document shredding by Andersen related to the Enron case, contains guidance related to audit documentation. Auditors must maintain audit documentation related to the auditor's report for seven years.

The interim audit standards remain in effect until the PCAOB has completed its review of standards. The ASB continues to have responsibility for setting auditing standards for audits of nonpublic companies. The relationship between the PCAOB and ASB for establishing auditing standards is still evolving, but it is likely that different standards will emerge for the audit of public and nonpublic companies. The General Accountability Office (GAO) continues to establish standards for the audits of governmental entities.

Accounting Standards

Similar to the requirements for auditing standards, Section 108 of the Sarbanes–Oxley Act specified criteria for accounting principles to be recognized as "generally accepted" by the SEC. In April 2003 the SEC announced that it will continue to recognize statements issued by the Financial Accounting Standards Board as being generally accepted. Section 109 of the Act provides that the accounting standards setting body be funded by the annual accounting support fee assessed against each public company.

Efforts are underway to make the FASB the sole accounting standard-setter. The GAAP hierarchy currently includes several different bodies with the authority to set standards. In addition to the FASB, the AICPA's Accounting Standards Executive Committee (AcSEC), the Emerging Issues Task Force (EITF) and the FASB staff have the ability to issue standards that are designated as authoritative. AcSEC currently has the ability to issue Statements of Position (SOPs), Industry Audit and Accounting Guides, and Practice Bulletins, all of which are included within the GAAP hierarchy. AcSEC will no longer be responsible for issuing authoritative standards and EITF consensuses will be subject to FASB approval.

Principles-Based Accounting Standards – A key issue in Enron was the so-called "3-percent rule" used to exclude special purpose entities from the consolidated financial statements of Enron. As a result, existing accounting standards received much criticism as being too rules-based and rewarding those willing to design transactions around the intent of the standards. Section 108(d) of the Act required the SEC to report on the feasibility of adopting a principles-based accounting system.

The SEC report suggests that a principles-based approach results in insufficient guidance to make the standards operational. The SEC recommends objective-oriented standards that charge management with capturing the economic substance of transactions and events as defined by substantive objectives built into each standard. These objectives would be based on the FASB's conceptual framework that emphasizes relevance, reliability, and comparability of data.

Most accounting transactions have both a balance sheet and income statement effect. In setting objectives-oriented standards, the SEC recommends an asset/liability view over a revenue/expense view. In the SEC's opinion, the scope of standards under a revenue/expense view tend to be defined at either too broad or too narrow a level. For example, revenue recognition is a significant accounting concern. Rather than write standards to address all the different conditions affecting revenue recognition, the SEC suggests that the focus of standards should be recognition of the related account receivable.

The move to objectives-oriented standards will also require improvements to the FASB's conceptual framework, as well as convergence with international standards. The following table outlines the action steps suggested by the SEC:

Key Steps Toward More Objectives-Oriented Accounting Standards

Action Items	Current Status	Time Horizon
Conceptual framework improvements project	FASB currently evaluating most efficient approach	Medium term
Move toward objectives-oriented form of standards	Recent standards (e.g., SFAS 141 and following) have more consistently included elements of objectives-oriented form	Immediate
Comprehensive review of current standards to identify and address those that are rules-based	Staff and Board evaluating existing standards for purposes of future agenda decisions	Underway
One standard setter	AcSEC will no longer be responsible for issuing "authoritative" standards, transition plan in place; EITF consensuses are now subject to FASB approval	Underway
Redefine GAAP hierarchy	Conceptual framework improvements project to be completed first	Medium term
Convergence	FASB and IASB jointly announce intention to work towards convergence of international and domestic standards	Underway, but effort will be long term

Source: http://www.sec.gov/news/studies/principlesbasedstand.htm

Quality Control

The PCAOB also has responsibility for quality control standards for auditors of public companies. The Public Oversight Board (POB) had been responsible for oversight of public company audits through its oversight of peer review and other regulatory programs of the SEC Practice Section of the AICPA. The POB voted to disband effective May 1,

2002 in response to plans by the SEC to reorganize the regulatory structure of public company audits following the Enron collapse and other perceived audit failures.

The PCAOB was declared operational by the SEC on April 25, 2003 and all accounting firms that "prepare or issue" or "participate" in the preparation of an audit report for an "issuer" were required to sign up with the PCAOB within 180 days of that date. An “issuer” is defined in the Sarbanes–Oxley Act, and includes public companies subject to SEC regulation under the Securities and Exchange Act of 1934 and issuers of securities under the Securities Act of 1933.

The PCAOB conducts inspections of registered accounting firms to assess the firm’s compliance with the rules of the PCAOB and SEC, professional standards, and the firm’s own quality control policies. Any violations could result in disciplinary action by the Board and reported to the SEC and state accountancy boards. Annual inspections are required for accounting firms that audit more than 100 issuers, and at least once every three years for other registered firms.

The PCAOB began its inspection program in 2003 with “limited procedure” inspections of the Big Four firms. The inspections focused on how the largest firms conducted selected audit engagements with an emphasis on professionalism and the “tone at the top.” In particular, the inspections focused on:

- How auditors made tough calls concerning the application of accounting principles in the financial statements.
- The accounting firm’s relationship and communications with the audit committee. Interviews with audit committee chairs have focused on such matters as the frequency and nature of discussion between the auditor and the audit committee; the audit committee’s expectations and evaluation of the auditor; and auditor communications regarding critical accounting judgments, including revenue recognition policies and related party transactions.

The initial reviews revealed perceptions by partners and staff of a renewed focus on audit quality. The PCAOB inspections provided some evidence consistent with this renewed focus in firm policies and how they are communicated within each audit firm. Nonetheless, the inspections identified significant audit and accounting issues. The PCAOB was particularly concerned that auditors may not place sufficient emphasis on the importance of thorough documentation of their work. The Sarbanes–Oxley Act specifically required the PCAOB to develop a standard on audit documentation, and information from the limited inspections was used in developing PCAOB Auditing Standard No. 3 on audit documentation.

The PCAOB will conduct full inspections of the largest U.S. firms in 2004, as well as many smaller audit firms. These inspections will focus on fraud detection; compliance with independence requirements; adequacy of documentation; identification, evaluation and management of risk; and compliance with auditing and accounting standards.

AUDITOR INDEPENDENCE

Non-Audit Services

Non-audit services, along with their potential effect on auditor independence, have long been a controversial issue for the accounting profession. Due to these independence concerns, the SEC had proposed prohibiting audit firms from providing any non-audit services to public company audit clients. Instead, the SEC issued revised rules on independence in 2000 that significantly restricted the ability of auditors to provide non-audit services to public company audit clients. However, the large amount of non-audit fees paid to Andersen by Enron again focused attention on the issue of non-audit services.

Section 201 of the Sarbanes–Oxley Act prohibits auditors from performing the nine categories of non-audit services included in the figure below for their public company audit clients. In addition, any non-prohibited services must be pre-approved by the audit committee. The SEC adopted rules strengthening auditor independence in January 2003 consistent with the requirements of Sarbanes–Oxley.

The Sarbanes–Oxley Act and the revised SEC rules restrict, but do not eliminate, the types of consulting services that can be offered to audit clients. Many of these services were prohibited under the existing SEC rules on independence adopted in November 2000. The new rules clarify many of the existing prohibitions, and expand the circumstances in which the services are prohibited. Some audit committees have concluded that they should not use their audit firm for any non-audit services, including tax services in many cases.

Restricted Consulting Services Under Sarbanes–Oxley and Revised SEC Rules

1. Bookkeeping and other accounting services
2. Financial information systems design and implementation
3. Appraisal or valuation services
4. Actuarial services
5. Internal audit outsourcing
6. Management or human resource functions
7. Broker or dealer or investment adviser, or investment banker services
8. Legal and expert services unrelated to the audit
9. Any other service that the PCAOB determines by regulation is impermissible

Four principles guide the SEC's application of principles of independence. Independence may be impaired if the relationship:

- Creates a mutual or conflicting interest between the accountant and audit client;
- Places the accountant in the position of auditing his or her own work;
- Results in the accountant acting as management or an employee of the audit client; or
- Places the accountant in a position of being an advocate for the audit client.

Tax Services – Recent events involving IRS investigations of tax shelters recommended by accounting firms and the provision of tax services to key employees at Sprint and other companies illustrate that tax services can create a potential conflict of interest for the auditor in which the firm is in essence auditing its own work. Several major companies have placed restrictions on the use of their outside audit firm for certain types of tax services.

The SEC has reiterated its long-standing position that an accounting firm can provide tax services to audit clients without impairing independence. As a result, accountants can continue to provide tax services such as tax compliance, tax planning, and tax advice to public company clients. However, these services must receive audit committee pre-approval. In addition, companies must disclose the amount of fees paid for tax services. The SEC noted that certain tax services could in certain circumstances impair independence. In particular, the SEC recommends that audit committees carefully scrutinize use of their audit firm for a transaction recommended by the accountant that may have tax avoidance as its sole purpose and whose tax treatment may not be supported by the Internal Revenue Code.

Although the SEC has indicated that tax services are generally allowed, the PCAOB has authority to establish auditor independence rules. The PCAOB has indicated that it will consider the impact of tax services on auditor independence, and convened a roundtable to review existing tax services provided by auditors to public company audit clients and discuss the effects these services may have on auditor independence.

Conflicts Arising from Employment Relationships

A company's employment of former audit team members raises independence concerns. Consistent with the requirements of Section 206 of the Sarbanes–Oxley Act, the SEC has added a one-year "cooling off" period before a member of the audit engagement team can work for the client in certain key management positions. This has important implications for an auditor working for a CPA firm who receives an employment offer from the client, if it is publicly held, for a position as a chief executive officer, controller, chief financial officer, chief accounting officer or equivalent position. The CPA firm cannot continue to audit that client if the auditor accepts the position and has participated in any capacity in the audit for one year preceding the start of the audit. This does not affect the CPA firm's ability to continue the audit if the former auditor accepts a position such as assistant controller or accountant without primary accounting responsibilities. This provision affects a public company's process of hiring for key financial reporting positions.

Under SEC rules before the Sarbanes–Oxley Act and continuing, an accounting firm is not independent with respect to an audit client if a former partner, principal, or shareholder, or professional employee of the firm accepts employment with a client if he or she has a continuing financial interest in the accounting firm, or is in a position to influence the accounting firm's operations or financial policies.

Partner Rotation

As required by the Sarbanes–Oxley Act, the SEC independence rules require that the lead and concurring partners rotate off the engagement after a period of five years. Although not addressed in the Act, the SEC requires a five-year "time out" for the lead and concurring partners after rotation before they can return to that audit client. Additional audit partners with significant involvement on the audit must rotate off after seven years and are subject to a two-year time out period.

GAO Study on Mandatory Audit Firm Rotation

The GAO issued a report in November 2003 on the potential effects of mandatory audit firm rotation as required by Section 207 of the Act. Mandatory rotation is advocated by those who believe that auditor independence is adversely affected by the audit firm's long-term relationship with the client. GAO surveys of the largest public accounting firms and Fortune 1000 publicly traded companies found that almost all believe that the costs of mandatory audit firm rotation are likely to exceed the benefits.

The GAO believes that mandatory auditor rotation may not be the most efficient way to strengthen auditor independence and improve audit quality. The GAO also believes several years' experience with the implementation of the Sarbanes–Oxley Act is needed before the effects of the Act can be assessed. The GAO suggests the best course of action is for the SEC and PCAOB to monitor and evaluate the effectiveness of existing requirements for enhancing auditor independence and audit quality. Several academic studies have been conducted to examine the effects of audit firm tenure. Most find evidence that longer audit firm tenure is associated with improved financial reporting quality, a finding consistent with the GAO's current position.

CHANGES IN THE CPA PROFESSION

Services Offered by Public Accounting Firms

The demise of Andersen following the firm's indictment for obstruction of justice in the Enron case, and the disposition of their consulting practices by three of the remaining Big 4 firms, have dramatically changed the face of the accounting profession.

The figure on the next page illustrates the relationship among the services offered by CPA firms. Over the past 20 years, consulting services increased in importance and eventually became the largest source of revenue for most of the largest firms. The disposition of consulting practices and restrictions on consulting services due to SEC regulations and the Sarbanes–Oxley Act have significantly reduced the importance of management consulting services to CPA firm practices.

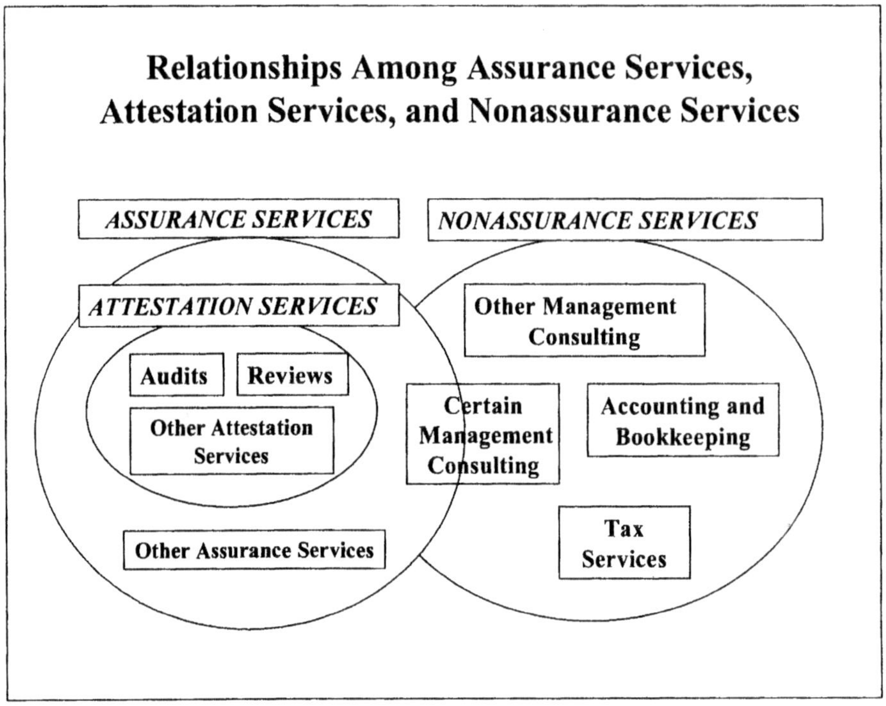

Source: *Auditing and Assurance Services: An Integrated Approach*, 10th Edition, A. Arens, R. Elder, and M. Beasley (p. 9)

It is important to emphasize that CPA firms continue to provide consulting and other business advisory services. However, the ability to offer these services to publicly held audit clients is significantly reduced. Tax services continue to be a significant source of revenue, but certain tax services are likely to be restricted for public company audit clients due to concerns that these services might impair auditor independence.

Dispositions and Other Changes in Major Firm Consulting Practices

Three of the Big 4 accounting firms, as well as the former Andersen firm, have sold or otherwise disposed of their consulting practices. These changes were partially due to independence concerns and restrictions placed on consulting practices. These changes originated well before passage of the Sarbanes–Oxley Act, and even before the SEC issued its revisions to auditor independence rules in November 2000. The following table summarizes the changes involving the consulting practices of the major international accounting firms.

Changes in Consulting Practices of Major Accounting Firms

Former Consulting Practice Name	Changes in Firm Name and Ownership
Andersen Consulting	• Separated from Andersen in August 2000 • Renamed Accenture in January 2001 • Became a public company in July 2001
Deloitte Consulting	• Announced plans to separate as a private partnership and change name to Braxton in 2002 • Terminated plans to separate from Deloitte & Touche in March 2003
Ernst & Young Consulting	• Sold to CapGemini in February 2000 • Consulting firm is known as CapGemini Ernst & Young but is not part of Ernst & Young
KPMG Consulting	• Completed initial public offering in February 2001 • Renamed BearingPoint in October 2002
PricewaterhouseCoopers Consulting	• Acquisition by IBM announced in July 2002

As illustrated in the table, only Deloitte & Touche has not disposed of its consulting practice. The Sarbanes–Oxley Act restricts the ability of CPA firms to offer consulting services to public company audit clients. However, CPA firms are not limited in the consulting services they can offer to private companies and public companies that are not audit clients, and can offer non-restricted services to publicly held audit clients. Deloitte & Touche has announced that they will retain their consulting practice, but still comply with the requirements of the Sarbanes–Oxley Act and the SEC's independence rules.

The first part of the table on the following page presents the ranking of the Big 4 accounting firms based on fiscal year 2003 revenue, along with information on the number of partners, professionals, U.S. offices, and mix of practice revenues. The second part of the table presents comparative data based on fiscal year 2000 information.

Because it has not disposed of its consulting practice, Deloitte & Touche is now the largest accounting firm, and derives more of its revenue from consulting than the other Big 4 firms. The comparative data indicate that the remaining Big 4 firms are smaller, and derive a much larger percentage of revenues from audit and attest services, and a much smaller percentage of revenues from consulting services. The fiscal year 2000 data indicates that Andersen was the fifth largest CPA firm. Prior to the separation of Andersen Consulting (now Accenture) in 2000, Andersen was the largest accounting firm, and derived 66 percent of its revenues from consulting.

Revenue and Other Data for the Largest CPA Firms in the United States

Fiscal Year 2003

Size by Revenue	Firm	Net Revenue – U.S. Only (in $ millions)	Partners	Professionals	U.S. Offices	Percentage of Total Revenue from Accounting and Auditing/Tax/ Management Consulting/Other
1	Deloitte & Touche	$6,511.0	2,613	20,487	91	39/25/27/9
2	Ernst & Young	$5,260.0	2,000	14,400	86	62/35/0/3
3	PricewaterhouseCoopers	$4,850.0	2,000	21,000	125	62/33/5/0
4	KPMG	$3,793.0	1,622	11,529	94	67/33/0/0

Source: *Accounting Today*: March 15-April 4, 2004/www.webcpa.com

Fiscal Year 2000

Size by Revenue	Firm	Net Revenue – U.S. Only (in $ millions)	Partners	Professionals	U.S. Offices	Percentage of Total Revenue from Accounting and Auditing/Tax/ Management Consulting
1	PricewaterhouseCoopers	$8,878.0	2,932	34,151	186	33/17/50
2	Deloitte & Touche	$5,838.0	2,155	20,658	103	31/19/50
3	KPMG	$5,400.0	1,500	19,000	145	35/22/43
4	Ernst & Young	$4,270.0	1,946	13,653	82	57/38/5
5	Andersen	$3,600.0	1,313	17,600	80	45/30/25

Source: *Accounting Today* ("The Electronic Accountant" - http://www.electronicaccountant.com/html/t100y2k/tocp3.htm)

GAO Study of Accounting Industry Consolidation

Section 701 of the Sarbanes–Oxley Act required the GAO to conduct a study on consolidation of public accounting firms. Before 1989 there were eight large accounting firms that were collectively known as the Big 8. During 1989, the Big 8 was reduced to the Big 6 after Ernst & Whinney merged with Arthur Young to form Ernst & Young, and Deloitte Haskins & Sells merged with Touche Ross to form Deloitte & Touche. Price Waterhouse merged with Coopers & Lybrand in 1998 to form PricewaterhouseCoopers, resulting in the Big 5. Finally, the demise of Andersen further reduced the Big 5 to the Big 4.

The GAO issued its report in July 2003. Several factors account for the consolidation trend, including globalization, the need for economies of scale, and the desire to build industry expertise. The resulting concentration has left large public companies with few choices in the selection of auditors. The GAO found that directly linking consolidation to changes in auditor fees, quality, or auditor independence is difficult, and that consolidation appeared to have little effect on capital formation or the securities markets to date. Finally, smaller accounting firms face significant barriers to entry in competing with the largest firms for public company audit clients. These barriers are even higher with the new registration and inspection processes now required by the PCAOB.

A second GAO report in September 2003 reported on a survey of large public companies. Respondents were mixed as to whether consolidation had influenced audit fees, but most believed that consolidation did not adversely impact audit quality or independence. Most respondents indicated that they would like greater choice in the number of large firms as they would not consider using a non-Big 4 firm, and were concerned about the impact of further consolidation. However, respondents did not advocate government intervention to increase competition.

CORPORATE RESPONSIBILITY

Role of the Audit Committee

Section 301 of the Act requires each member of the audit committee to be an independent member of the board of directors. In addition, Section 407 requires public companies to disclose whether at least one member of its audit committee is a financial expert as defined in the Act. The figure on the next page describes ways audit committee members can satisfy the financial expert requirements. The audit committee is to be directly responsible for the appointment, compensation, and oversight of the work of the auditor, including the approval of any non-audit services.

The national stock exchanges have also made recent changes to the listing requirements for companies whose securities trade on those exchanges. For example, the New York Stock Exchange changed listing requirements designed to strengthen corporate governance and disclosure. Among the many changes, the NYSE now requires the chair of the audit committee of NYSE registrants to have accounting or financial management experience, and listed companies must have an audit committee, nominating committee, and compensation committee each comprised solely of independent directors. Furthermore, NYSE registrants must also have an internal audit function.

Ways for an Audit Committee Member to Become a "Financial Expert"

- Education and experience as a principal financial officer, principal accounting officer, controller, public accountant or auditor or experiences in one or more positions that involve the performance of similar functions;
- Experience actively supervising the principal financial officer, principal accounting officer, controller, public accountant, auditor or person performing similar functions;
- Experience overseeing or assessing the performance of companies or public accountants with respect to the preparation, auditing, or evaluation of financial statements; or
- Other relevant experience.

Responsibility for Financial Statements

Management has always been responsible for the financial statements. The Sarbanes–Oxley Act increases management's responsibility by requiring the chief executive officer (CEO) and chief financial officer (CFO) of public companies to certify the quarterly and annual financial statements submitted to the SEC. By signing those statements, management is certifying that the financial statements fully comply with the requirements of the Securities Exchange Act of 1934 and that the information contained in the report fairly presents, in all material respects, the financial condition and results of operations.

While financial statements filed with the SEC have previously included management's signatures, the significance of the new CEO and CFO certifications is greatly enhanced. Sarbanes–Oxley contains criminal penalties for anyone who knowingly falsely certifies those statements. To avoid these possibilities, most CEOs and CFOs of public companies now devote significant time to due diligence procedures conducted with other members of the management team before signing the certifications at each quarter and year end. The figure on the next page summarizes the six elements of management's certification.

An example of the certification from Harley-Davidson, Inc.'s chief executive officer for the company's annual statements filed in the Form 10-K with the SEC is included on page 16. That example illustrates specific statements made by the chief executive officer related to each of the required elements of the certification. The CEO will make similar statements in the quarterly financial statements submitted in Form 10-Q's. In addition, the Forms 10-Q and 10-K filed with the SEC will contain similar certifications (not shown here) from Harley-Davidson's chief financial officer. In addition to CEO and CFO certifications of both quarterly and annual financial statements, auditors are responsible for performing reviews of the quarterly financial statements before they are filed with the SEC.

Six Elements of Management's Certification of Financial Statements

1. Management has reviewed the financial statements.

2. Based on management's knowledge, the financial statements do not contain any untrue material fact or omit to state a material fact.

3. Based on management's knowledge, the financial statements and other financial information fairly present in all material respects the financial condition, results of operations, and cash flows of the company as of and for the period presented.

4. Management
   a. Is responsible for establishing and maintaining disclosure controls and procedures of the company.
   b. Has designed such disclosure programs and controls to ensure that material information is made known to them, particularly during the period in which the report is being prepared.
   c. Has evaluated the effectiveness of the company's disclosure controls and procedures as of a date within 90 days prior to the filing date of the report.
   d. Has presented in the report containing the financial statements their conclusions about the effectiveness of those disclosure controls and procedures based on the required evaluation as of that date.

5. Management has disclosed to its auditors and the audit committee
   a. All significant deficiencies in the design or operation of internal control, which could adversely affect the company's ability to record, process, summarize and report financial data and have identified for the auditors any material weaknesses in internal controls.
   b. Any fraud, whether or not material, that involves management or other employees who have a significant role in the issuer's internal controls.

6. Management has indicated in the report containing the financial statements whether or not there were significant changes in internal controls or in other factors that could significantly affect internal controls subsequent to the date of management's evaluation, including any corrections to address significant deficiencies and material weaknesses.

Penalty Provisions

The responsibilities of the CEO and CFO are reinforced by various penalty provisions in the Act. A CEO or CFO who certifies financial statements that they know do not fully comply with SEC requirements can result in a fine of not more than $5 million and/or imprisonment up to 20 years.

If the financial statements are required to be restated due to material misconduct, the CEO and CFO must return any bonus or other incentive-based compensation, as well as profits from the sale of company stock, received during the 12-month period following initial issuance of the financial statements requiring restatement.

Chief Executive Officer Certification

I, Jeffrey L. Bleustein, certify that:

1. I have reviewed this annual report on Form 10-K of Harley-Davidson, Inc.;

2. Based on my knowledge, this annual report does not contain any untrue statement of a material fact or omit to state a material fact necessary to make the statements made, in light of the circumstances under which such statements were made, not misleading with respect to the period covered by this annual report;

3. Based on my knowledge, the financial statements, and other financial information included in this annual report, fairly present in all material respects the financial condition, results of operations and cash flows of the registrant as of, and for, the periods presented in this annual report;

4. The registrant's other certifying officer and I are responsible for establishing and maintaining disclosure controls and procedures (as defined in Exchange Act Rules 13a-14 and 15d-14) for the registrant and have:

   a) designed such disclosure controls and procedures to ensure that material information relating to the registrant, including its consolidated subsidiaries, is made known to us by others within those entities, particularly during the period in which this annual report is being prepared;

   b) evaluated the effectiveness of the registrant's disclosure controls and procedures as of a date within 90 days prior to the filing date of this annual report (the "Evaluation Date"); and

   c) presented in this annual report our conclusions about the effectiveness of the disclosure controls and procedures based on our evaluation as of the Evaluation Date;

5. The registrant's other certifying officer and I have disclosed, based on our most recent evaluation, to the registrant's auditors and the audit committee of the registrant's board of directors (or persons performing the equivalent functions):

   a) all significant deficiencies in the design or operation of internal controls which could adversely affect the registrant's ability to record, process, summarize and report financial data and have identified for the registrant's auditors any material weaknesses in internal controls; and

   b) any fraud, whether or not material, that involves management or other employees who have a significant role in the registrant's internal controls; and

6. The registrant's other certifying officer and I have indicated in this annual report whether there were significant changes in internal controls or in other factors that could significantly affect internal controls subsequent to the date of our most recent evaluation, including any corrective actions with regard to significant deficiencies and material weaknesses.

Date: March 28, 2003
Jeffrey L. Bleustein
Chief Executive Officer

REPORTS ON PUBLIC COMPANY INTERNAL CONTROL

Prior to the issuance of the Sarbanes–Oxley Act, some public companies voluntarily issued reports on internal control, and such reports were required by regulators in certain industries, such as banking. Perceived failures in internal control over financial reporting led Congress to include provisions in the Sarbanes–Oxley Act for required management reporting on internal controls over financial reporting for *all* public companies.

Section 404 of the Sarbanes–Oxley Act directed the SEC to prescribe rules to require management of all public companies to issue an "internal control report" in its annual report that includes the following:

- A statement that management is responsible for establishing and maintaining an adequate internal control structure and procedures for financial reporting
- An assessment of the effectiveness of the internal control structure and procedures for financial reporting as of the end of the company's fiscal year

Section 404 also requires that the company's auditor attest to and issue a report on management's assessment of internal control. PCAOB Standard No. 2 issued in March 2004 contains guidance for the audit of internal control over financial reporting for public companies.

In June 2003, the SEC issued rules to comply with the Section 404 provisions. Public companies with market capitalization over $75 million must comply with the reporting requirements for fiscal years ending on or after November 15, 2004. All other public companies must comply for their fiscal years ending on or after July 15, 2005.

Management and auditors of public companies are devoting extensive efforts to meet the reporting requirements of Section 404. The SEC deferred implementation deadlines twice in recognition of the complexity of satisfying the reporting and auditing requirements. While companies have long recognized the importance of strong internal controls, most companies have not maintained the necessary documentation and evaluation procedures that mandatory public reporting on internal control by both management and their auditor requires. Thus, most public companies are spending significant time and resources to ensure that they are prepared for the extensive Section 404 reporting requirements.

Management's Responsibility for Internal Control

The SEC's rules regarding the implementation of Section 404 require management's report on internal control be included in its annual report (i.e., Form 10-K) filed with the SEC. Management's report on internal control must include the following:

- A statement of management's responsibility for establishing and maintaining adequate internal control over financial reporting;
- Management's assessment of the effectiveness of the company's internal controls over financial reporting as of the end of the company's most recent fiscal year end (e.g., the balance sheet date);

- A statement identifying the framework used by management to evaluate the effectiveness of internal control over financial reporting; and
- A statement that the auditor of the company's financial statements has issued an attestation report on management's report on internal control over financial reporting.

To satisfy these requirements, management is obligated to maintain evidence and other forms of documentation to provide reasonable support for their assertions about internal control. Despite the fact that effective internal control may be functioning, the lack of adequate documentation of the performance of those controls leaves management with little, if any, basis for concluding that their internal controls over financial reporting are operating effectively. In fact, the SEC believes that developing and maintaining such evidence is an inherent element of effective internal control. Thus, the establishment of documentation of the functioning of internal control is a critical responsibility of management.

Definition of Internal Control – The SEC's rules regarding the certification of internal control define internal control over financial reporting as a process designed by or under the supervision of the company's chief executive and chief financial officers to provide reasonable assurance regarding the reliability of financial reporting and the preparation of financial statements for external purposes in accordance with generally accepted accounting principles and includes policies and procedures that:

- Pertain to the maintenance of records that in reasonable detail accurately and fairly reflect the transactions and dispositions of the assets of the company;
- Provide reasonable assurance that transactions are recorded as necessary to permit preparation of financial statements in accordance with generally accepted accounting principles, and receipts and expenditures of the company are being made only in accordance with authorizations of management and directors of the company; and
- Provide reasonable assurance regarding prevention or timely detection of unauthorized acquisition, use or disposition of company assets that could have a material effect on the financial statements.

COSO Internal Control Framework – Under the SEC's final rules, management's report must identify the framework used to evaluate the effectiveness of internal control. The framework must be a recognized control framework established by a body or group that followed a due-process procedure that allows for public comment. The internal control framework for most U.S. companies will be the Committee of Sponsoring Organizations of the Treadway Commission's (COSO's) *Internal Control – Integrated Framework.*

COSO's internal control framework, issued in 1992, is the most widely used and understood framework in the U.S. As illustrated in the figure on the following page, the framework establishes three broad categories of controls: effectiveness and efficiency of operations; reliability of financial reporting; and compliance with laws and regulations. It also identifies five interrelated components of effective internal control that apply to each category of controls: control environment, risk assessment, control activities, information and communications, and monitoring.

The scope of the Section 404 reporting requirements encompasses the five interrelated components of internal control that relate to financial reporting. Internal controls over financial reporting include those related to COSO's reliability of financial reporting category plus those controls related to the operations and compliance with laws and regulations categories that could materially affect financial reporting.

Committee of Sponsoring Organizations Internal Control Framework

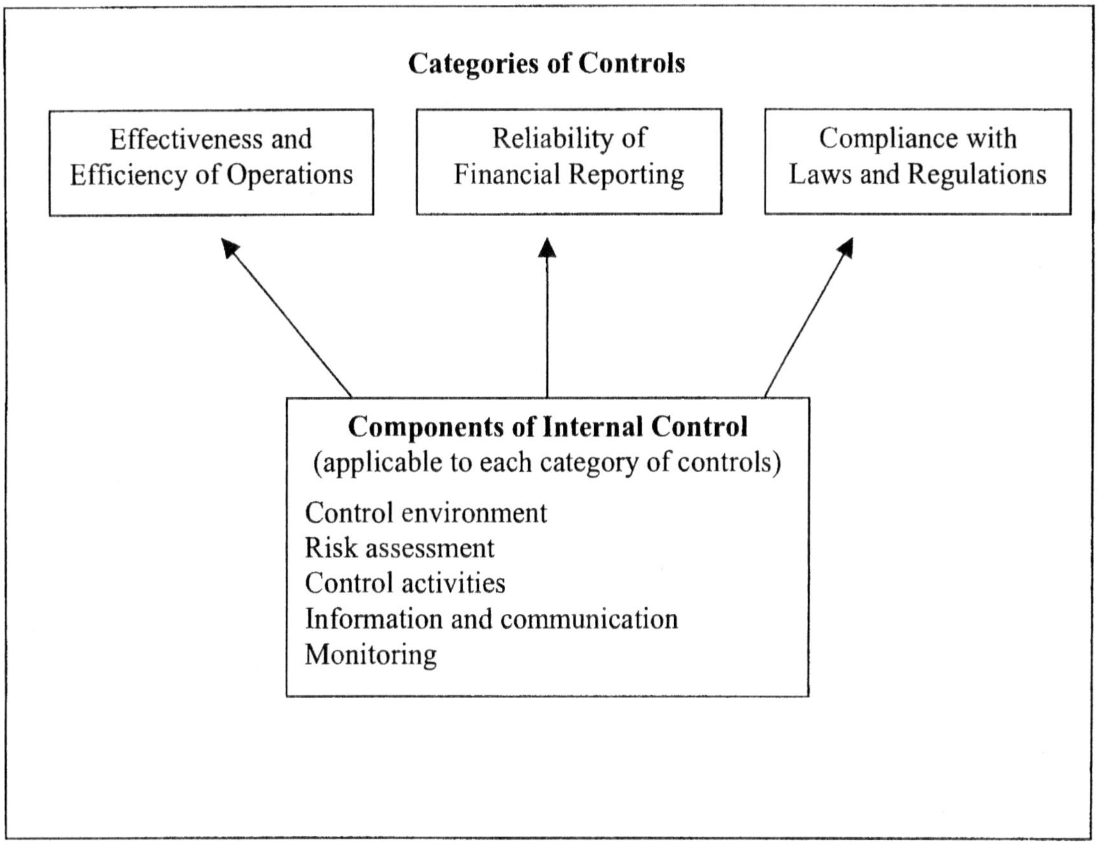

Management's Internal Control Assessment

Management's assessment of internal control over financial reporting consists of two key components. First, management must evaluate the *design* of internal control over financial reporting. Second, management must test the *operating effectiveness* of those controls.

Design of Internal Control - When evaluating the design of internal control over financial reporting, management evaluates whether the control is designed to prevent or detect material misstatements in the financial statements. Management's focus is on controls over all relevant assertions related to all significant accounts and disclosures in the financial statements. As part of the assessment, management evaluates information about how significant transactions are initiated, authorized, recorded, processed, and reported to identify points in the flow of transactions where material misstatements due to error or fraud could occur. Management must determine whether existing controls would be effective if they operated as designed and whether all the necessary controls are in place.

The types of information gathered by management to assess design effectiveness might take many forms, including policy manuals, flowcharts, narratives, documents and other forms that are in either paper or electronic formats. Management "walkthroughs" of controls will confirm the controls' design and whether they have been placed in operation. The form and content of information documented by management varies depending on the size of the company and the nature and complexity of the business. Management's failure to maintain adequate documentation about the design of controls is considered to be a deficiency in the company's internal control.

Operating Effectiveness of Controls - In addition to evaluating the design of internal control over financial reporting, management must test the operating effectiveness of controls. The testing objective is to determine whether the control is operating as designed and whether the person performing the control possesses the necessary authority and qualifications to perform the control effectively. Test results, which must also be documented, form the basis for management's assertion at the end of the fiscal year about the controls' operating effectiveness.

The nature of management's tests of operating effectiveness will include a mix of inquiries of personnel, inspection of relevant documentation, observation of the company's operations, and reperformance of the application of the controls. Tests of controls will be conducted over a period of time to be able to adequately determine whether the controls are operating effectively. For example, the timing of tests of controls performed daily will differ from the timing of tests of controls performed monthly or quarterly. Testing in earlier periods also allows management time to implement corrective actions, if necessary, before auditor testing of controls occurs.

Management's natural starting point is the evaluation of internal controls at the entity level, given their pervasive effect on the organization. For example, hiring policies, ethical codes of conduct, management's reporting philosophy and operating style affect the overall corporate environment or culture in which financial reporting occurs. Information about entity-level internal controls helps determine whether management has created a control environment in which people are motivated to comply with controls and whether the company has implemented necessary control mechanisms to monitor and correct non-compliance. Without effective internal controls at the entity level, the best policies and procedures at account or transaction levels will be worthless.

Once management's evaluation of controls at the entity level is complete, management's evaluation centers around business processes and controls that relate to relevant assertions for significant accounts. An account or group of accounts is significant if an error in the account could individually or when aggregated with others materially affect the financial statements. Assertions that are relevant to significant accounts include those assertions having a meaningful bearing on whether the account is fairly stated. These generally include assertions related to the account's valuation, existence, completeness, and presentation and disclosure.

Identification of Internal Control Deficiencies

Management's process of evaluating the design and operating effectiveness of internal controls over financial reporting may reveal deficiencies. There are three categories of deficiencies that might exist:

- ***Control deficiency*** - Exists when the design or operation of a control does not allow management or employees, in the normal course of performing their assigned functions, to prevent or detect misstatements on a timely basis.
- ***Significant deficiency*** - Exists if there is more than a remote likelihood that internal controls will fail to prevent or detect misstatements that are larger than inconsequential. A control deficiency is considered to be significant when the deficiency adversely affects the company's ability to initiate, authorize, record, process, or report external financial data reliably in accordance with generally accepted accounting principles.
- ***Material weakness*** - Exists if a significant deficiency, by itself, or in combination with other significant deficiencies, results in more than a remote likelihood that internal controls will fail to prevent or detect material financial statement misstatements.

The primary difference between a significant deficiency and a material weakness is the materiality of the potential misstatement. Examples of circumstances that are at least significant deficiencies and strong indicators of material weaknesses include restatements of prior period financial statements, the identification by auditors of material misstatements in financial statements, and fraud of any magnitude on the part of senior management.

Depending on the timing of tests of controls, management might be able to implement changes in the company's controls to make them more effective or efficient and to address control deficiencies. Changes made to address control deficiencies may or may not affect management's assertion about control design or operating effectiveness. Sufficient time following the change must be available to permit management to re-assess the design and operating effectiveness of controls following the change prior to auditor testing.

Management Reporting

Management's annual report filed with the SEC must include an assessment of the effectiveness of the company's controls over financial reporting in addition to its audited financial statements as of the end of the most recent fiscal year. A required element of the report is management's written conclusion about the effectiveness of the company's internal control over financial reporting. If there is one or more material weakness, management will be unable to conclude that the company's internal control over financial reporting is effective and must disclose all material weaknesses that exist as of the end of the most recent fiscal year.

Management's conclusion about internal control may not be affected by material weaknesses discovered earlier during the period as long as controls have been changed to eliminate the material weakness sufficiently in advance of the end of the fiscal period to allow adequate testing of the changed control.

In addition to providing a written conclusion about internal control over financial reporting, management must also disclose to the auditor all deficiencies in the design or operation of internal control over financial reporting identified by management. This includes separate disclosure of all significant deficiencies and material weaknesses.

Audits of Internal Control Over Financial Reporting

In addition to requiring management reports on internal control over financial reporting, Section 404 of the Sarbanes–Oxley Act also requires that the company's auditor attest to and issue a report on management's assessment of internal control. PCAOB Auditing Standard No. 2 contains guidance for the audit of internal control over financial reporting for public companies.

The objective of an audit of internal control over financial reporting is to form an opinion as to whether management's assessment of the design and operating effectiveness of internal control over financial reporting is fairly stated in all material respects. This not only involves evaluating management's assessment process, but it also involves the auditor arriving at his or her own independent assessment of the internal control's design and operating effectiveness.

PCAOB Auditing Standard No. 2 requires that the audit of internal control over financial reporting be performed by the same audit firm conducting the audit of the company's financial statements. The PCAOB's intent is that work performed for the audit of internal control be integrated with the work performed for the audit of the financial statements. The PCAOB decided that these audits should be integrated because the objectives of and the work involved in performing an audit of internal control over financial reporting and an audit of the financial statements are closely related.

In an audit of the financial statements, the auditor obtains an understanding of internal controls in every audit to assess control risk. Under PCAOB Auditing Standard No. 2, auditors will continue to obtain an understanding of internal controls in every audit of the financial statements to assess control risk. However, they will perform other procedures to report on management's assertion about internal controls.

Understanding internal controls and tests of controls performed solely for the purpose of expressing an opinion on the financial statements are not sufficient for the purpose of expressing an opinion on internal controls. In an audit of the financial statements, auditors obtain an understanding of internal control to assess control risk. When control risk is assessed below the maximum, the auditor designs and performs a combination of tests of controls and substantive procedures. When control risk is assessed at maximum, the auditor performs substantive procedures only. As a result, the range of controls tested varies based on the auditor's assessment of control risk.

Differences in Scope of Controls Tested in an Audit of Internal Control and an Audit Financial Statements

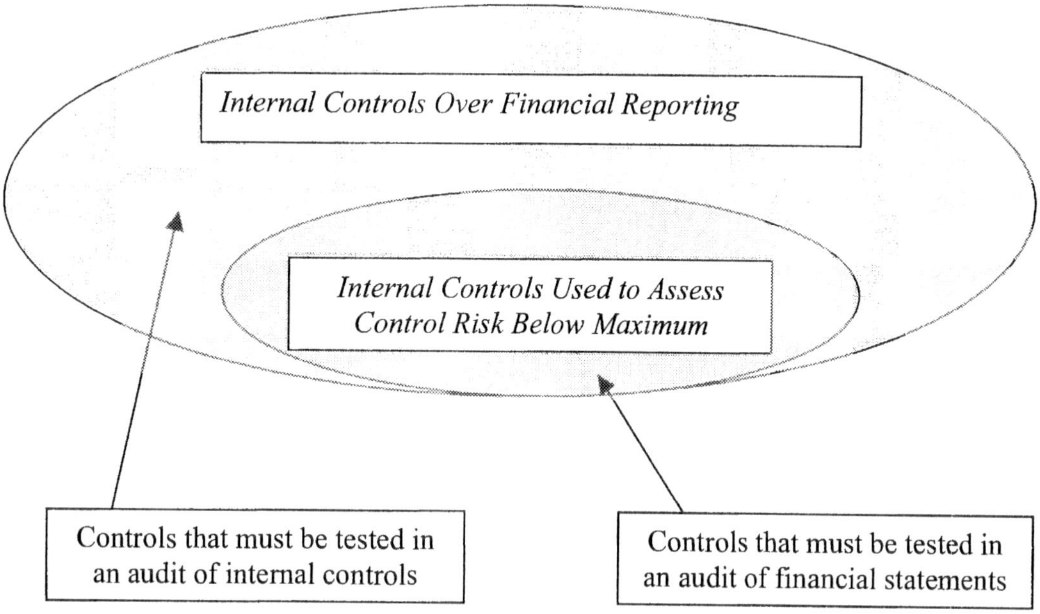

Source: *Auditing and Assurance Services: An Integrated Approach*, 10th Edition, A. Arens, R. Elder, and M. Beasley (p. 295)

In contrast, the range of controls to be tested by auditors to express an opinion on internal controls is significantly broader than that tested solely to express an opinion on the financial statements. To express an opinion on internal controls, the auditor obtains an understanding of and performs tests of controls related to *all* significant account balances, classes of transactions, and disclosures and related assertions in the financial statements. Those controls may not be tested in a financial statement audit. The figure above illustrates the differences in controls tested in an audit of internal controls from controls tested in an audit of the financial statements.

The level of assurance obtained from tests of controls in an audit of internal controls differs from the level of assurance obtained from tests of controls in an audit of financial statements. Tests of controls performed in an audit of internal control should be sufficient to obtain a high level of assurance about their operating effectiveness. Test of controls performed in a financial statement audit may only provide moderate or low assurance about their operating effectiveness, given that other assurance is obtained from substantive procedures. Thus, the nature, timing, and extent of those tests of controls are likely to be greater than tests of controls performed in a financial statement audit. The figure on the following page illustrates the differences in the types of procedures performed to serve as the basis for the opinion on internal controls and the opinion on the financial statements.

Comparison of Audit of Internal Controls and Audit of Financial Statements

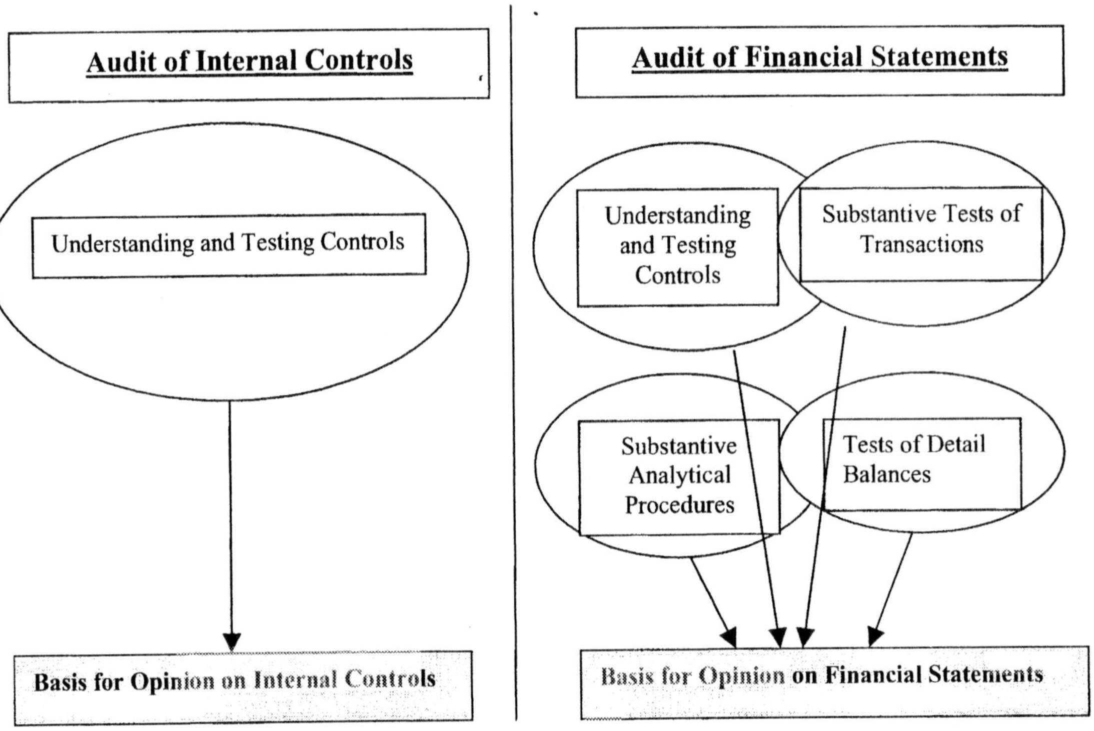

While the nature, timing and extent of testing controls differ between an audit of the financial statements and the audit of internal controls, auditors can use the knowledge about internal controls obtained as part of the audit of internal controls as the basis for the understanding of internal control in an audit of the financial statements. Similarly, auditors may consider the results of tests of controls performed in the audit of internal controls, as well as internal control deficiencies identified, when assessing control risk and designing substantive procedures for the financial statement audit.

Because of the inherent limitations of internal control, the degree of reliance that can be placed by the auditor on internal control to reduce the likelihood of material misstatements in the financial statements is limited, regardless of the effectiveness of internal control. Auditors of the financial statements must continue to perform substantive procedures for each material account and class of transactions. The extent of evidence obtained about the operating effectiveness of internal controls in an audit of internal controls does not eliminate the requirement for the auditor to perform substantive procedures in the financial statement audit.

Evidence the auditor obtains from performing substantive procedures in an audit of the financial statements should be considered by the auditor when auditing internal controls. When substantive procedures detect material misstatements, the auditor should consider whether that evidence affects judgments about the effectiveness of internal controls. Material misstatements detected by the auditor that were not identified by the client ordinarily indicate the existence of a material weakness in internal control.

One likely change in the audit of public companies as a result of the requirement for the audit of internal controls is an increased reliance on internal controls in financial statement audits. Previously, it was often cost effective to perform increased substantive tests instead of tests of controls in some or all cycles even if controls were effective. The auditor is now likely to rely on these controls because they must be tested in the audit of internal controls.

Auditor's Report on Audit of Internal Control Over Financial Reporting

The auditor's report on the audit of internal control over financial reporting may be issued separately or combined with the report on the audit of the financial statements. Because the audit of the financial statements and management's assertion about internal control is an integrated activity, the date of the auditor's opinion on the financial statements and the auditor's opinion on internal control should be the same. Note that the report, in addition to referring to the report on management's assertion on internal control, includes an additional paragraph on inherent limitations of internal control. The opinion on the financial statements addresses multiple reporting periods on the financial statements. For management's assertion about the effectiveness of internal control, the report is as of the end of the most recent fiscal period. The following page provides an example of a combined report.

OTHER FINANCIAL DISCLOSURES

Loans to Executives

Because of the lack of independence between the parties involved, Section 402 of the Sarbanes–Oxley Act prohibits related party transactions that involve personal loans to executives. It is now unlawful for any public company to extend or maintain credit, to arrange for the extension of credit, or to renew the extension of credit in the form of a personal loan to any director or executive officer of the company. These restrictions do not apply to any loan, such as a home loan or credit card agreement, made by a bank or other insured financial institution under normal banking operations using market terms offered to the general public.

Code of Ethics for Senior Financial Officers

Companies frequently communicate the entity's values and ethical standards through policy statements and codes of conduct. In response to Section 406 requirements in the Sarbanes–Oxley Act, the SEC now requires each public company to disclose whether it has adopted a code of ethics that applies to senior management, including the CEO, CFO, and principal accounting officer or controller. A company that has not adopted such a code must disclose this fact and explain why it has not done so. The SEC also requires companies to promptly disclose amendments and waivers to the code of ethics related to any of those officers. The figure on page 27 summarizes the standards that should be included in a public company's code of ethics.

Sample Combined Report on Financial Statements and Internal Control

Independent Auditor's Report

Introductory Paragraph

We have audited the accompanying balance sheets of Westbrook Company, Inc. as of December 31, 2004 and 2003, and the related statements of income, stockholders' equity and comprehensive income, and cash flows for each of the years in the three-year period ended December 31, 2004. We have also audited management's assertion included in the accompanying management report on internal control that Westbrook Company, Inc. maintained effective internal control over financial reporting as of December 31, 2004, based on criteria established in *Internal Control-Integrated Framework* issued by the Committee of Sponsoring Organizations of the Treadway Commission (COSO). Westbrook Company's management is responsible for these financial statements, for maintaining effective internal control over financial reporting, and for its assessment of the effectiveness of internal control over financial reporting. Our responsibility is to express an opinion on these financial statements, an opinion on management's assessment, and an opinion on the effectiveness of the company's internal control over financial reporting based on our audits.

Scope Paragraph

We conducted our audits in accordance with the standards of the Public Company Accounting Oversight Board (United States). Those standards require that we plan and perform the audits to obtain reasonable assurance about whether the financial statements are free of material misstatement and whether effective internal control over financial reporting was maintained in all material respects. Our audit of financial statements included examining, on a test basis, evidence supporting the amounts and disclosures in the financial statements, assessing the accounting principles used and significant estimates made by management, and evaluating the overall financial statement presentation. Our audit of internal control over financial reporting included obtaining an understanding of internal control over financial reporting, evaluating management's assessment, testing and evaluating the design and operating effectiveness of internal control, and performing such other procedures as we considered necessary in the circumstances. We believe that our audits provide a reasonable basis for our opinions.

Definition Paragraph

A company's internal control over financial reporting is a process designed to provide reasonable assurance regarding the reliability of financial reporting and the preparation of financial statements for external purposes in accordance with generally accepted accounting principles. A company's internal control over financial reporting includes those policies and procedures that (1) pertain to the maintenance of records that, in reasonable detail, accurately and fairly reflect the transactions and dispositions of the assets of the company; (2) provide reasonable assurance that transactions are recorded as necessary to permit preparation of financial statements in accordance with generally accepted accounting principles, and that receipts and expenditures of the company are being made only in accordance with authorizations of management and directors of the company; and (3) provide reasonable assurance regarding the prevention or timely detection of unauthorized acquisition, use, or disposition of the company's assets that could have a material effect on the financial statements.

Inherent Limitations Paragraph

Because of its inherent limitations, internal control over financial reporting may not prevent or detect misstatements. Also, projections of any evaluation of effectiveness to future periods are subject to the risk that internal control may become inadequate because of changes in conditions, or that the degree of compliance with the policies or procedures may deteriorate.

Opinion Paragraph

In our opinion, the financial statements referred to above present fairly, in all material respects, the financial position of Westbrook Company, Inc. as of December 31, 2004 and 2003, and the results of its operations and its cash flows for each of the years in the three-year period ended December 31, 2004 in conformity with accounting principles generally accepted in the United States of America. Also in our opinion, management's assessment that Westbrook Company maintained an effective internal control over financial reporting as of December 31, 2004, is fairly stated, in all material respects, based on criteria established in *Internal Control-Integrated Framework* issued by the Committee of Sponsoring Organizations of the Treadway Commission (COSO). Furthermore, in our opinion, Westbrook Company maintained, in all material respects, effective internal control over financial reporting as of December 31, 2004, based on criteria established in *Internal Control-Integrated Framework* issued by the Committee of Sponsoring Organizations of the Treadway Commission (COSO).

Johnson and Wilson, LLP
March 6, 2005

Required Elements of the Code of Ethics

A Code of Ethics must include written standards that are reasonably designed to deter wrongdoing and to promote:

- Honest and ethical conduct, including the ethical handling of actual or apparent conflicts of interest between personal and professional relationships;
- Full, fair, accurate, timely, and understandable disclosure in reports and documents that a public company files with the SEC or includes in other public communications;
- Compliance with applicable governmental laws, rules, and regulations;
- Prompt internal reporting to an appropriate person identified in the code of violations of the code; and
- Accountability for adherence to the code.

Audit Committee Discussions with Auditors

Section 204 of the Sarbanes–Oxley Act requires the auditor to timely report on the following items to the audit committee:

- All critical accounting policies and practices to be used.
- All alternative treatments of financial information within generally accepted accounting principles that have been discussed with management, ramifications of the use of such alternative disclosures and treatments, and the treatment preferred by the auditor.
- Other material written communications between the auditor and management, such as a management letter or schedule of unadjusted audit differences.

As the audit is completed, the audit committee should obtain from the auditor information about the initial selection of and changes in significant accounting policies or their application during the current audit period. When changes have occurred, the auditor should inform the committee of the reasons for the change. The auditor should also communicate information about methods used to account for significant unusual transactions and the effect of significant accounting policies in controversial or emerging areas.

SAS NO. 99, *CONSIDERATION OF FRAUD IN A FINANCIAL STATEMENT AUDIT*

The issuance of the Sarbanes–Oxley Act of 2002 represents a direct response by Congress to the high-profile financial reporting frauds at Enron and WorldCom, among others. Much of the focus of the Act is centered on the role of the external auditor.

Within in five months of the passage of the Act, the AICPA Auditing Standards Board (ASB) issued SAS No. 99, *Consideration of Fraud in Financial Statement Audit*. The standard superseded SAS No. 82 in providing guidance to auditors in fulfilling their responsibility as it relates to fraud in an audit of financial statements. Although the occurrence of several high-profile alleged cases of fraudulent financial reporting provided primary motivation for the issuance of the Sarbanes–Oxley Act, the ASB's efforts to issue SAS No. 99 were well underway before the issuance of the Act.

The following section provides an overview of the key provisions contained in SAS No. 99. While auditors do have fraud detection responsibilities, other corporate governance participants, such as management, boards of directors, audit committees, internal auditors, and many others also play a vital role in the prevention and detection of material misstatements due to fraud. The guidance in SAS No. 99, while directly applicable to auditors, provides useful information to all corporate governance participants interested in preventing fraudulent financial reporting.

Errors Versus Fraud

SAS 99 distinguishes between two types of misstatements: errors and fraud. Either type of misstatement can be material or immaterial. An *error* is an *unintentional* misstatement of the financial statements, whereas *fraud* is *intentional*. Two examples of errors are a mistake in extending price times quantity on a sales invoice and overlooking older raw materials in determining the lower of cost or market for inventory.

For fraud, there is a distinction between *misappropriation of assets*, often called defalcation or employee fraud, and *fraudulent financial reporting*, often called management fraud. An example of misappropriation of assets is a clerk taking cash at the time a sale is made and not entering the sale in the cash register. An example of fraudulent financial reporting is the intentional overstatement of sales near the balance sheet date to increase reported sales and earnings.

Auditing standards make no distinction between the auditor's responsibility for searching for errors and fraud, whether from fraudulent financial reporting or misappropriation of assets. For both errors and fraud, the auditor must obtain reasonable assurance about whether the statements are free of material misstatements.

The standards also recognize that it is often more difficult to detect fraud than errors because management or the employees perpetrating the fraud *attempt to conceal the fraud*. The difficulty of detection does not change the auditor's responsibility to properly plan and perform the audit.

Auditor Fraud Detection Responsibility

The auditor's SAS No. 99 responsibility for detecting material misstatements due to fraud is as follows:

> *"The auditor has a responsibility to plan and perform the audit to obtain reasonable assurance about whether the financial statements are free of material misstatement, whether caused by error or fraud."*

Assessing Fraud Risks

To meet their fraud detection responsibilities, auditors obtain information to assess the risk of fraud arising from fraudulent financial reporting and misappropriations of assets. Auditors gather information to determine the extent that fraud conditions exist. There are three conditions of fraud described in SAS No. 99. These include the following:

1. *Incentives/Pressures.* Management or other employees have incentives or pressures to commit fraud.
2. *Opportunities.* Circumstances provide opportunities for management or employees to commit fraud.
3. *Attitudes/Rationalization.* An attitude, character, or set of ethical values exist that allow management or employees to commit a dishonest act or they are in an environment that imposes sufficient pressure that causes them to rationalize committing a dishonest act.

These three conditions are often referred to as the "fraud triangle," which is illustrated below.

The Fraud Triangle

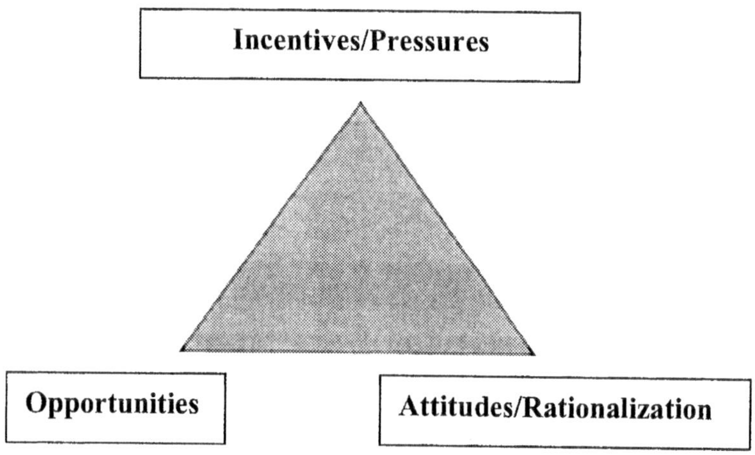

Source: *Auditing and Assurance Services: An Integrated Approach*, 10th Edition, A. Arens, R. Elder, and M. Beasley (p. 312)

Forensic experts believe the evaluation of information about fraud is enhanced when it is considered in the context of these three conditions. Considering the possibility of fraud along these dimensions provides a helpful framework for obtaining and evaluating information about the risks of material misstatements due to fraud. The table on the following page provides examples of fraud risk factors for each of the three conditions of fraud for fraudulent financial reporting.

Information Affecting Risk of Fraud

Auditors have historically used fraud risk factor checklists as their primary source of information about fraud risks. Based on the belief that auditor processes for identifying and assessing fraud risks needed to be improved, SAS No. 99 significantly expanded the requirements and guidance for gathering information about the risks of fraud. The emphasis is on obtaining a broader set of information as the source of input about fraud risks that is beyond simply considering fraud risk factors. Considering all information about risks, not just the risk factors, should improve the auditor's ability to identify and assess those risks, and aid in designing appropriate audit procedures.

Auditors now consider the following:

- Specific risk factors related to fraudulent financial reporting and misappropriations of assets.
- Information obtained from experienced audit team members about their knowledge of the company and its industry, including how and where the company might be susceptible to material misstatements due to fraud.
- Responses to auditor inquiries of management about their views of the risks of fraud and about existing programs and controls to address specific identified fraud risks.
- Analytical procedures results obtained during planning that indicate possible implausible or unexpected analytical relationships.
- Knowledge obtained through such things as client acceptance and retention decisions, interim review of financial statements, and the consideration of fraud risks.

The auditor considers all the information gathered through the performance of these procedures in the context of the three conditions present when fraud exists: incentives/pressures, opportunities, and attitudes/rationalization. The figure on page 32 summarizes how the auditor uses all the information gathered to assess fraud risks.

Communications among Engagement Personnel - As depicted in the figure, a dialogue held among the audit team about fraud risks that might be present serves as one of the sources of information auditors use to assess fraud risks. SAS No. 99 requires the audit team to conduct these discussions to share insights from more experienced audit team members and "brainstorm" ideas that address the following:

Examples of Risk Factors for Fraudulent Financial Reporting

THREE CONDITIONS OF FRAUD

Incentives/Pressures	**Opportunities**	**Attitudes/Rationalization**
Management or other employees have incentives or pressures to materially misstate financial statements.	*Circumstances provide an opportunity for management or employees to misstate financial statements.*	*An attitude, character, or set of ethical values exists that allows management or employees to intentionally commit a dishonest act, or they are in an environment that imposes sufficient pressure that causes them to rationalize committing a dishonest act.*
Examples of Risk Factors	**Examples of Risk Factors**	**Examples of Risk Factors**
• Financial stability or profitability is threatened by economic, industry, or entity operating conditions. Examples include significant declines in customer demand and increasing business failures in either the industry or overall economy. • Excessive pressure for management to meet debt repayment or other debt covenant requirements. • Management or the board of directors' personal net worth is materially threatened by the entity's financial performance.	• Significant accounting estimates involve subjective judgments or uncertainties that are difficult to verify. • Ineffective board of director or audit committee oversight over financial reporting. • High turnover or ineffective accounting, internal audit, or information technology staff.	• Inappropriate or ineffective communication and support of the entity's values. • Known history of violations of securities laws or other laws and regulations. • Management's practice of making overly aggressive or unrealistic forecasts to analysts, creditors, and other third parties.

Source: Auditing and Assurance Services: An Integrated Approach, 10th Edition, A. Arens, R. Elder, and M. Beasley (p. 313).

Sources of Information Gathered to Assess Fraud Risks

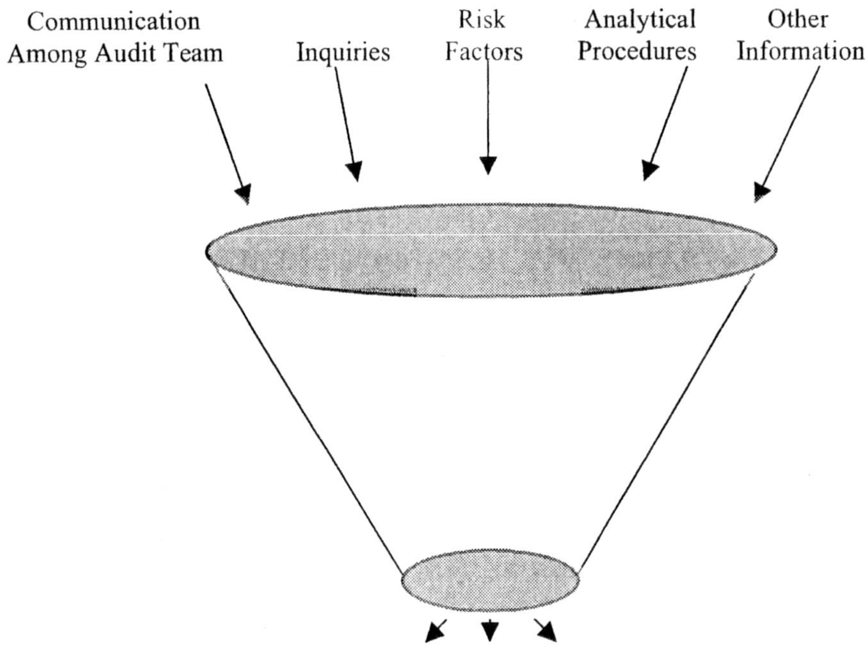

Identified Risks of Material Misstatements Due to Fraud

Source: *Auditing and Assurance Services: An Integrated Approach*, 10th Edition, A. Arens, R. Elder, and M. Beasley (p. 316)

- How and where they believe the entity's financial statements might be susceptible to material misstatement due to fraud. This should include consideration of known external and internal factors affecting the entity that might
  - Create an incentive or pressure for management to commit fraud.
  - Provide the opportunity for fraud to be perpetrated.
  - Indicate a culture or environment that enables management to rationalize fraudulent acts.
- How management could perpetrate and conceal fraudulent financial reporting.
- How assets of the entity could be misappropriated.
- How the auditor might respond to the susceptibility of material misstatements due to fraud.

Focus on Professional Skepticism - SAS No. 1 states that, in exercising professional skepticism, an auditor *"neither assumes that management is dishonest nor assumes unquestioned honesty."* In practice, maintaining this attitude of "neutrality" can be difficult because, despite allegations in some recent high profile cases, material frauds are still relatively rare in relation to number of audits of financial statements conducted annually. In fact, most auditors will never encounter a material fraud during their careers. Also, through rigorous client acceptance and continuance evaluation procedures, auditors reject most potential clients perceived as lacking appropriate levels of honesty and integrity.

SAS No. 99 places stronger emphasis on the auditor's consideration of a client's susceptibility to fraud, regardless of the auditor's beliefs about the likelihood of fraud and management's honesty and integrity. Specifically, the standard requires that during audit planning in every audit, the engagement team must discuss the need to maintain a questioning mind throughout the audit in identifying fraud risks and to critically evaluate audit evidence.

- **Questioning Mind:** In maintaining a "questioning mind" auditors should set aside any prior beliefs about management's integrity and honesty. In this regard, the discussion should include consideration of the potential for management override of controls.
- **Critical Evaluation of Audit Evidence:** Auditors should thoroughly probe the issues, acquire additional evidence as necessary, and consult with other team members rather than rationalize or dismiss information or other conditions that indicate a material misstatement due to fraud may have occurred.

Similar to auditors of financial statements, other participants in the corporate governance process need to use an appropriate level of professional skepticism as they consider the risk of fraud in the financial statements. All should recognize that fraud is possible in any client.

Responding to the Risks of Fraud

When risks of material misstatements due to fraud are identified, the auditor should first discuss these findings with management and obtain management's views of the potential fraud and existing programs and controls designed to prevent or detect misstatements. Management may have programs and controls designed to mitigate specific risks of fraud or broader programs designed to prevent, deter, and detect fraud.

Auditors consider whether such programs and controls mitigate the identified risks of material misstatements due to fraud or whether specific control deficiencies exacerbate the risks. When assessing the risks of material misstatement due to fraud, the auditor considers whether programs and controls are suitably designed and placed in operation.

SAS No. 99 describes the three ways auditors respond to fraud risks as including the following:

1. Design and perform audit procedures to address identified risks.
2. Change the overall conduct of the audit to respond to identified fraud risks.
3. Perform procedures to address the risk of management override of controls.

The last of these three responses recognizes that the risk of management override of controls exists in virtually all audits and can manifest itself in a number of unpredictable ways. Because management is in a unique position to perpetrate fraud by overriding established controls that would otherwise appear to be operating effectively, auditors must now perform procedures in every audit to further address the risk of management override of controls. Three procedures must be performed in every audit:

1. **Examining journal entries and other adjustments for evidence of possible misstatements due to fraud.** SAS No. 99 requires testing of journal entries and other financial statement adjustments because fraud often involves the recording of inappropriate or unauthorized journal entries throughout the year or at period end and adjustments to amounts reported in the financial statements that are not reflected in formal journal entries. The auditor is required to:

    - Obtain an understanding of the entity's financial reporting process and the controls over journal entries and other adjustments.
    - Identify and select journal entries and other adjustments for testing.
    - Determine the timing of the testing.
    - Inquire of individuals involved in the financial reporting process about inappropriate or unusual activity relating to the processing of journal entries and other adjustments.

2. **Reviewing accounting estimates for biases.** Fraudulent financial reporting is often accomplished through intentional misstatement of accounting estimates. SAS No. 99 requires the auditor to consider the potential for management bias when reviewing current year estimates. It requires a "look back" at significant prior year estimates to look for any changes in the company's process or management's judgments and assumptions that might indicate a potential bias. For example, management's estimates may have been clustered at the high end of the range of acceptable amounts in the prior year and clustered at the low end of the range in the current year.

3. **Evaluate the business rationale for significant unusual transactions.** SAS No. 99 places greater focus on understanding the underlying business rationale for significant unusual transactions that might be outside the normal course of business for the company, given the auditor's understanding of the entity and its environment. The auditor should gain an understanding of the business rationale and whether that rationale suggests that the transactions have been entered into to engage in fraudulent financial reporting.

Evaluating Audit Evidence

The auditor's assessment of the risks of material misstatement due to fraud should be ongoing throughout the audit. Conditions may be identified during fieldwork that change or support a judgment about the assessment of fraud risks. For example, the auditor should be alert for the following conditions:

- Discrepancies in the accounting records.
- Conflicting or missing evidential matter.
- Problematic or unusual relationships between the auditor and management.

- Results from substantive or final review stage analytical procedures that indicate a previously unrecognized fraud risk.
- Responses to inquiries made throughout the audit that have been vague or implausible, or that have produced evidence that is inconsistent with other evidence.

CONCLUSION

The impact of the Sarbanes–Oxley legislation and related rules issued by the SEC, PCAOB, and other standards setters is tremendous. These new provisions are already having a significant effect on auditors and other participants in the corporate governance process for public companies. Many observers are already describing a significant "trickle-down effect" whereby many of the provisions of the Act are being considered for organizations other than public companies, such as private enterprises, not-for-profit, and government entities. Thus, the impact of the Act and related regulatory and standards-setting changes is wide-sweeping.

It may take several years before there is sufficient information to determine whether these provisions actually result in a reduced number of instances of fraudulent financial reporting. Many argue that the costs of compliance far exceed the anticipated benefits of the new legislation. What is certain, however, is that the provisions are affecting all aspects of public financial statement reporting and should not be taken lightly by any involved.

ASSIGNMENT MATERIAL

Review Questions

1. What types of entities are subject to the provisions of the Sarbanes–Oxley Act of 2002?

2. What is the authority of the newly created Public Company Accounting Oversight Board (PCAOB)?

3. Who is responsible for establishing auditing standards for audits of public companies? Who is responsible for establishing accounting standards for public companies? Explain.

4. Describe how the issuance of the Sarbanes–Oxley Act affects accounting standards setting in the United States.

5. Discuss what is meant by an "objectives-oriented" approach to accounting standards setting.

6. To what extent do the Sarbanes–Oxley Act and revised SEC independence rules expand the types of consulting services that impair auditor independence? What consulting services are not allowed under the Sarbanes–Oxley Act?

7. Under what circumstances may a public company engage its auditor to perform tax services? When might tax services impair auditor independence?

8. Explain why several large accounting firms disposed of their consulting practices. Did the Sarbanes–Oxley Act play a role in these decisions?

9. What is the largest source of revenue for the Big 4 accounting firms? What was likely the largest source of revenue for these firms before the year 2000?

10. When can a public company hire a member from its audit firm's engagement team?

11. Briefly describe the arguments for and against mandatory audit firm rotation.

12. What types of attributes should an audit committee member possess to be deemed a "financial expert"?

13. Who is responsible for certifying the financial statements filed with the SEC and how often will the certifications be made?

14. How does the restatement of prior period financial statements affect CEO and CFO personal compensation?

15. What internal control framework is most likely to be used by U.S. public companies to satisfy the Section 404 provisions of the Sarbanes–Oxley Act?

16. What are the two key components of management's assessment of internal control over financial reporting? How do they differ?

17. How does the lack of documentation of the performance of internal controls potentially affect management's report on internal control over financial reporting?

18. In a report on internal control, does the auditor's report cover internal control for a period or at a point of time? What date should be used for the auditor's report on internal control?

19. How long must auditors retain audit documentation?

20. Who is considered as "the client" when auditing public companies?

21. Which services must be pre-approved by the audit committee?

22. Which types of loans to executives are permitted by the Sarbanes–Oxley Act?

23. What is the auditor's reporting responsibility related to the client's internal controls?

24. Explain how the scope of internal controls tested by the auditor in an audit of the financial statements differs from controls tested by the auditor in an audit of internal controls.

25. What types of audit procedures does the auditor perform to provide a basis for the auditor's report on internal control?

26. Describe matters that the auditor must communicate to the audit committee of public companies.

27. What are the three conditions of fraud often referred to as "the fraud triangle?"

28. What sources are used by the auditor to gather information to assess fraud risks?

29. What are the three categories of auditor responses to fraud risks?

30. What procedures must the auditor perform to address the risk of management override of controls?

Multiple Choice

1. Which of the following is *not* a general principle used by the SEC in evaluating the effect of other services on auditor independence?
   a. An auditor cannot function in the role of management.
   b. The fee for the additional services must be less than the audit fee.
   c. An auditor cannot audit his or her own work.
   d. An auditor cannot serve in an advocacy role for the client.

2. In which of the following situations would an audit firm be considered not independent with respect to a public company audit client under the provisions of the Sarbanes–Oxley Act?
   a. The client hires an audit firm member as its CFO. The CFO left the audit firm one month earlier, and participated in the most recent audit of the company.
   b. The audit firm provides tax planning services to the client. The services were pre-approved by the audit committee.
   c. The lead audit partner for the client has served in that capacity for the past four years.
   d. The audit firm provides general business consulting services that were pre-approved by the audit committee.

3. Which of the following would prohibit management from being able to certify the annual financial statements?
   a. The chief financial officer is not a CPA.
   b. There are deficiencies, although not significant, in internal control.
   c. Management has not evaluated the effectiveness of its internal controls within the last six months.
   d. Management has no knowledge of any untrue material facts contained in the financial statements.

4. Which of the following control deficiencies would automatically prohibit management from concluding that internal control over financial reporting is operating effectively?
   a. The presence of any type of control deficiency, regardless of significance.
   b. Only the presence of significant deficiencies.
   c. The presence of one or more material weaknesses.
   d. The presence of either a significant deficiency or a material weakness.

5. The SEC requires public companies to
   a. Disclose waivers made to the code of ethics for senior management.
   b. Have a code of ethics.
   c. Include a "financial expert" on the audit committee.
   d. Appoint a CPA as chair of the audit committee.

6. When providing an opinion on internal controls, the auditor
   a. Performs tests of a broader range of controls than those tested in the financial statement audit.
   b. Uses the understanding and testing of internal controls performed in the audit of the financial statements as the basis for the opinion on internal controls.
   c. Must only test controls when control risk is assessed below the maximum.
   d. Performs a combination of tests of controls and substantive procedures, including tests of details of balances.

7. Which of the following is an example of the "incentives/pressures" fraud condition?
   a. Selected financial statement ratios are not in compliance with covenants in bank loan documents.
   b. Material account balances are dependent on management estimation.
   c. Senior executives frequently waive internal control provisions.
   d. The majority of the board of directors consists of management.

Problems

1. The following situations involve the provision of non-audit services. Indicate whether the service is a violation of the requirements of the Sarbanes–Oxley Act and SEC rules.
   a. Providing bookkeeping services to a public company. The services were pre-approved by the audit committee of the company.
   b. Providing internal audit services to a public company that is not an audit client.
   c. Designing and implementing a financial information system for a private company.
   d. Recommending a tax shelter to a client that is publicly-held. The services were pre-approved by the audit committee.
   e. Providing internal audit services to public company client with the pre-approval of the audit committee.
   f. Providing bookkeeping services to an audit client that is a private company.

2. During audit planning, the auditor obtained the following information:
   a. Management has a strong interest in employing inappropriate means to minimize reported earnings for tax-motivated reasons.
   b. Assets and revenues are based on significant estimates that involve subjective judgments and uncertainties that are hard to corroborate.
   c. The company is marginally able to meet exchange listing and debt covenant requirements.
   d. Significant operations are located and conducted across international borders in jurisdictions where differing business environments and cultures exist.
   e. There are recurring attempts by management to justify marginal or inappropriate accounting on the basis of materiality.
   f. The company's financial performance is threatened by a high degree of competition and market saturation.

   Classify each of the six factors into one of these fraud conditions: incentives/pressures; opportunities; or attitudes/rationalization.

APPENDIX

SUMMARY OF KEY PROVISIONS OF THE SARBANES–OXLEY ACT

TITLE I – PUBLIC COMPANY ACCOUNTING OVERSIGHT BOARD

Section 101: Establishment; Administrative Provisions – The Public Company Oversight Board ("the Board") will have five financially-literate members, appointed for five-year terms. Two of the members must be or have been certified public accountants, and the remaining three must not be and cannot have been CPAs.

Section 102: Registration with the Board – Audit firms involved in the audits of public companies must register with the Board.

Section 103: Auditing, Quality Control, and Independence Standards and Rules – The Board will establish auditing and related attestation standards, quality control standards, and ethics standards to be used by registered accounting firms in the preparation and issuance of audit reports of issuers as required by the Act and SEC rules. The Board will include in auditing standards a requirement that registered accounting firms prepare and maintain working papers for a period of at least seven years.

Section 104: Inspections of Registered Public Accounting Firms – Annual quality control inspections must be conducted every year for firms that audit more than 100 issuers. Other firms must be inspected at least once every 3 years. Special inspections may be requested by the SEC or Board.

Section 105: Investigations and Disciplinary Proceedings – If the Board determines that any registered firm has engaged in practices in violation of the Sarbanes–Oxley Act ("the Act"), the rules of the Board, or securities laws related to the issuance of audit reports, the Board may impose sanctions, including temporary suspension or permanent revocation of registration or association of individuals with a registered firm, monetary penalties, censure, additional education or training, or other sanctions provided by the rules of the Board.

Section 106: Foreign Public Accounting Firms – Foreign public accounting firms that prepare an audit report for an issuer are subject to the Act and oversight of the PCAOB. This may include foreign firms that do not issue an audit report but are responsible for performing some of the audit work, such as auditing a foreign subsidiary, that is relied on by the primary auditor.

Section 107: Commission Oversight of the Board – The Securities and Exchange Commission (SEC) shall have oversight and enforcement authority over the Board. No rule of the Board shall become effective without prior approval of the SEC.

Section 108: Accounting Standards

Section 108(b): Recognition of Accounting Standards – The SEC may recognize as "generally accepted" for purposes of the securities laws any accounting principles established by a standard setting body that:

- is organized as a private entity;
- has a board of trustees or equivalent body, the majority of whom are not or have not been associated persons of a registered accounting firm for the past two years;
- is funded by an accounting support fee assessed against issuers;
- has adopted procedures to ensure prompt consideration of changes to accounting principles by a majority vote;
- considers, when adopting standards, the need to keep them current and the extent to which international convergence of standards is necessary or appropriate.

Section 108(d): Study and Report on Adopting Principles-Based Accounting – Within one year of enactment of the Act, the SEC shall report on the feasibility of adopting a principles-based accounting system.

Section 109: Funding – The PCAOB and accounting standard setting body shall be funded by an annual accounting support fee to be assessed against each issuer.

TITLE II – AUDITOR INDEPENDENCE

Section 201: Services Outside the Scope of Practice of Auditors – It is unlawful for a registered public accounting firm to provide non-audit services to an issuer, including: (1) bookkeeping or other services related to the accounting records or financial statements of the audit client; (2) financial information systems design and implementation; (3) appraisal or valuation services, fairness opinions, or contribution-in-kind reports; (4) actuarial services; (5) internal audit outsourcing services; (6) management functions or human resources; (7) broker or dealer, investment adviser, or investment banking services; (8) legal services and expert services unrelated to the audit; (9) any other service that the Board determines, by regulation, is impermissible.

Other non-audit services may be provided if they are pre-approved by the audit committee. The audit committee will disclose to investors in periodic reports its decision to preapprove non-audit services.

Section 202: Preapproval Requirements – All audit services and non-audit services provided by the auditor shall be preapproved by the audit committee.

Section 203: Audit Partner Rotation – The lead audit or coordinating partner and the reviewing partner must rotate off of the audit every 5 years.

Section 204: Auditor Reports to Audit Committees – The accounting firm must report to the audit committee all: 1) critical accounting policies and practices to be used; 2) all alternative treatments of financial information within GAAP that have been discussed with management, ramifications of the use of such alternative disclosures and treatments, and the treatment preferred by the accounting firm.

Section 205: Conforming Amendments – Amends the Securities Exchange Act of 1934 to define the term 'audit committee' as "a committee (or equivalent body) established by and amongst the board of directors of an issuer for the purpose of overseeing the accounting and financial reporting processes of the issuer and audits of the financial statements of the issuer." The term "independent public account" is replaced by the term "registered public accounting firm."

Section 206: Conflicts of Interest – The CEO, Controller, CFO, Chief Accounting Officer or person in an equivalent position cannot have been employed by the company's audit firm during the 1-year period preceding the audit.

Section 207: Study of Mandatory Rotation of Registered Public Accountants – The GAO will do a study on the potential effects of requiring the mandatory rotation of audit firms.

TITLE III – CORPORATE RESPONSIBILITY

Section 301: Public Company Audit Committees – Each member of the audit committee shall be an independent member of the board of directors of the issuer. The audit committee will be directly responsible for the appointment, compensation, and oversight of the work of any registered public accounting firm employed by the issuer.

Section 302: Corporate Responsibility For Financial Reports – The CEO and CFO of each issuer shall certify in each annual or quarterly report that: 1) they have reviewed the report; 2) based on their knowledge, the report does not contain any untrue statement or omit any material facts; 3) based on the their knowledge, the financial statements and disclosures fairly present in all material respects the operations and financial condition of the issuer; 4) that the officers are responsible for establishing and maintaining internal controls and have evaluated the effectiveness of internal controls; 5) they have disclosed to the auditors and audit committee all sighificant deficiencies in the design or operations of internal controls, and any fraud, whether or not material, that involves management or other employees with a significant role in the company's internal controls; and 6) any significant changes in internal controls subsequent to their evaluation of the controls.

Section 303: Improper Influence on Conduct of Audits – It shall be unlawful for any officer or director of an issuer to take any action to fraudulently influence, coerce, manipulate, or mislead any auditor engaged in the performance of an audit for the purpose of making the financial statements materially misleading.

Section 304: Forfeiture of Certain Bonuses and Profits – If an issuer is required to issue restated financial statements due to material misconduct resulting in noncompliance with any financial reporting requirement under the securities laws, the chief executive officer and chief financial officer shall reimburse the issuer for any bonus or other incentive-based or equity-based compensation received from the issuer, as well as any profits realized from sale of securities of the issuer, during the 12-month period following the issuance of the financial statements found to be in noncompliance.

Section 306: Insider Trades During Pension Blackout Periods – Prohibits the purchase or sale of stock by officers and directors and other insiders during blackout periods. Any profits from sales in violation of this section shall inure to and are recoverable by the issuer.

Section 307: Rules of Professional Responsibility for Attorneys – The SEC shall issue rules setting forth minimum standards of conduct for attorneys appearing and practicing before the SEC in any way in the representation of issuers. The rules shall require an attorney to report evidence of a material violation of securities law or breach of fiduciary duty or similar violation by the company or any of its agents to the chief legal counsel or the chief executive officer of the company. If the counsel or CEO does not respond appropriately to the evidence, the attorney shall report the evidence to the audit committee of the board of directors.

Section 308: Fair Funds for Investors – If the SEC obtains a civil penalty against any person in addition to an order requiring disgorgement for a violation of securities laws or related rules and regulations, the civil penalty shall at the discretion of the SEC be added to the disgorgement fund for the benefit of the victims of the violation.

TITLE IV – ENHANCED FINANCIAL DISCLOSURES

Section 401: Disclosures in Periodic Reports

Section 401(a) - Each financial report that is required to be prepared in accordance with GAAP shall reflect all material correcting adjustments that have been identified by a registered accounting firm.

Each annual and quarterly financial report shall disclose all material off-balance sheet transactions and other relationships with unconsolidated entities that may have a material current or future effect on the financial condition of the issuer.

Section 401(b) - The SEC shall issue rules providing that pro forma financial information must be presented so as not to contain an untrue statement or omit to state a material fact that would make the pro forma financial information misleading, and that pro forma information must be reconciled with the financial condition and results of operations of the issuer under generally accepted accounting principles.

Section 401(c) – Within one year of adoption of off-balance sheet disclosure rules, the SEC shall study off-balance sheet disclosures to determine (a) the extent of off-balance sheet transactions; and (b) whether generally accepted accounting rules result in the financial statement of issuers reflecting the economics of off-balance sheet transactions to investors in a transparent fashion. Within six months of completion of the study, the SEC shall report to Congress with recommendations to improve the transparency and quality of reporting off-balance sheet transactions.

Section 402: Enhanced Conflict of Interest Provisions - Generally, it will be unlawful for an issuer to extend credit to any director or executive officer. Consumer credit companies may make home improvement and consumer credit loans and issue credit cards to its directors and executive officers if it is done in the ordinary course of business on the same terms and conditions made to the general public.

Section 403: Disclosures of Transactions Involving Management and Principal Stockholders - Directors, officers, and 10% owners must report designated transactions by the end of the second business day following the day on which the transaction was executed.

Section 404: Management Assessment of Internal Controls – Requires the annual report of each issuer to include an internal control report which shall:

(1) state the responsibility of management for establishing and maintaining an adequate internal control structure and procedures for financial reporting; and

(2) contain an assessment, as of the end of the issuer's fiscal year, of the effectiveness of the internal control structure and procedures of the issuer for financial reporting.

The internal control report is to be attested to by the auditor as part of the audit engagement.

Section 406: Code of Ethics for Senior Financial Officers – Each issuer must disclose whether it has adopted a code of ethics for senior financial officers, and the reasons if it has not adopted a code of ethics. The company must immediately disclose any change in or waiver of the code of ethics for senior financial officers.

Section 407: Disclosure of Audit Committee Financial Expert –The SEC shall issue rules to require issuers to disclose whether at least 1 member of its audit committee is a financial expert as defined in Section 407 of the Act.

Section 408: Enhanced Review of Periodic Disclosures by Issuers – The SEC shall review disclosures by issuers. In scheduling reviews, the SEC shall consider: (1) issuers that have issued material restatements of financial results; (2) issuers that experience significant volatility in their stock price; (3) issuers with the largest market capitalization; (4) emerging companies with disparities in price to earnings ratios; (5) issuers whose operations significantly affect any material sector of the economy; and (6) any other factors that the SEC may consider relevant.

Section 409: Real Time Disclosure – Issuers must disclosure information on material changes in the financial condition or operations of the issuer "in plain English" on a rapid and current basis.

TITLE V – ANALYST CONFLICTS OF INTEREST

Section 501: Treatment of Securities Analysts by Registered Securities Associations – National securities exchanges and registered securities associations must adopt conflict of interest rules for research analysts who recommend equities in research reports.

TITLE VI – COMMISSION RESOURCES AND AUTHORITY

Section 601: Authorization of Appropriations – SEC appropriations for 2003 were increased, including $98 million to hire an additional 200 employees to provide enhanced oversight of auditors and audit services.

Section 602: Appearance and Practice Before the Commission - The SEC may censure any person, or temporarily bar or deny any person the right to appear or practice before the SEC if the person does not possess the requisite qualifications to represent others, lacks character or integrity, or has willfully violated Federal securities laws. With respect to any registered accounting firm, improper professional conduct means: (1) intentional or knowing conduct, including reckless conduct, that results in a violation of professional standards; and (2) negligent conduct in the form of (a) a single instance of highly unreasonable conduct that results in a violation of professional standards; or (b) repeated instances of unreasonable conduct, each resulting in a violation of professional standards.

TITLE VII – STUDIES AND REPORTS

Section 701: GAO Study and Report Regarding Consolidation of Public Accounting Firms – The GAO will conduct a study to identify the factors that have led to the consolidation of accounting firms since 1989, the impact of the consolidation on capital formation and securities markets, and solutions to any problems identified, including ways to increase competition and the number of firms capable of providing audit services to large business organizations subject to the securities laws.

Section 702: Commission Study and Report Regarding Credit Rating Agencies – The SEC will conduct a study of the role and function of credit rating agencies in the function of the securities markets.

Section 703: Study and Report on Violators and Violations – The SEC will conduct a study of the period January 1, 1998 to December 31, 2001 to determine the number of securities professionals, defined as public accountants, public accounting firms, investment bankers, investment advisers, brokers, dealers, attorneys, and other professionals practicing before the SEC, found to have violated or aided and abetted a violation of the securities laws, as well as a description of the securities law violations.

Section 704: Study of Enforcement Actions – The SEC shall review and report to Congress on all enforcement actions by the SEC involving violations of reporting requirements imposed under the securities laws and restatements of financial statements over the 5-year period preceding enactment of the Act.

Section 705: Study of Investment Banks – The Comptroller General of the United States will conduct a study on whether investment banks and financial advisers assisted public companies in manipulating their earnings.

TITLE VIII – CORPORATE AND CRIMINAL FRAUD ACCOUNTABILITY

Section 801: Short Title – The title may be referred to as the "Corporate and Criminal Fraud Accountability Act of 2002".

Section 802: Criminal Penalties for Altering Documents – It is a felony to knowingly destroy or create documents to impede, obstruct or influence any existing or contemplated federal investigation. Auditors are required to maintain all audit or review work papers for five years after the end of the fiscal period audited.

Section 806: Protection for Employees of Publicly Traded Companies Who Provide Evidence of Fraud – Employees of issuers and accounting firms are extended whistleblower protection that would prohibit the employer from discharging or taking other action against employees who lawfully disclose information which the employee reasonably believes constitutes a violation of securities laws or Federal law relating to fraud against shareholders.

Section 807: Criminal Penalties for Defrauding Shareholders of Publicly Traded Companies – Anyone who knowingly defrauds shareholders of a publicly traded company shall be fined, imprisoned not more than 25 years, or both.

TITLE IX – WHITE-COLLAR CRIME PENALTY ENHANCEMENTS

Section 901: Short Title – The title may be referred to as the "White-Collar Crime Penalty Enhancement Act of 2002".

Section 903: Criminal Penalties for Mail and Wire Fraud – The maximum penalties for mail fraud and wire fraud are increased from five years to 20 years.

Section 905: Amendment to Sentencing Guidelines Relating to Certain White-Collar Offenses – The United States Sentencing Commission shall review and, as appropriate, amend the Federal Sentencing guidelines and related policy statements to implement the provisions of the Act.

Section 906: Failure of Corporate Officers to Certify Financial Reports – The CEO and CFO must certify that the financial statements and disclosures fully comply with provisions of the Securities Exchange Act and that they fairly present, in all material respects, the operations and financial condition of the issuer. Maximum penalties for willful certification of the financial statements knowing that they do not fully comply with the requirements are a fine of not more than $5,000,000 and/or imprisonment of up to 20 years.

TITLE X – CORPORATE TAX RETURNS

Section 1001: Sense of the Senate Regarding the Signing of Corporate Tax Returns by Chief Executive Officers – It is the sense of the Senate that the Federal income tax return of a corporation should be signed by the chief executive officer.

TITLE XI – CORPORATE FRAUD AND ACCOUNTABILITY

Section 1101: Short Title – The title may be referred to as the "Corporate Fraud Accountability Act of 2002".

Section 1102: Tampering With a Record or Otherwise Impeding an Official Proceeding – Any person who corruptly alters, destroys, mutilates, or conceals any record, document or other object with the intent to impair the object's integrity or availability for use in an official proceeding or to otherwise obstruct, influence or impede any official proceeding shall be fined and/or imprisoned for up to 20 years

Section 1103: Temporary Freeze Authority for the Securities and Exchange Commission – The SEC is authorized to freeze the payment of any extraordinary payment to any director, officer, partner, controlling person, agent, or employee of a company during an investigation of possible violations of securities laws.

Section 1104: Amendment to the Federal Sentencing Guidelines – The United States Sentencing Commission is requested to promptly review the sentencing guidelines applicable to securities and accounting fraud and related offenses. The Sentencing Commission is requested to ensure that the sentencing guidelines and policy statements reflect the serious nature of these offenses and the need for aggressive and appropriate law enforcement action to prevent such offenses.

Section 1105: Authority of the Commission to Prohibit Persons from Serving as Officers and Directors – The SEC may prohibit a person from serving as an officer or director of a public company if the person has committed securities fraud.

Section 1106: Increased Criminal Penalties Under Securities Exchange Act of 1934 – The maximum penalty for individuals under the 1934 Act is increased from a fine of $1,000,000, or imprisonment for not more than 10 years, to a fine of $5,000,000, or imprisonment for not more than 20 years. The maximum fine on corporations is increased from $2,500,000 to $25,000,000.

Section 1107: Retaliation Against Informants – Any individual who knowingly retaliates or takes any action harmful to any person providing information relating to the commission or possible commission of any Federal offense, shall be fined or imprisoned not more than 10 years, or both.

The full text of the Sarbanes–Oxley Act can be accessed through the AICPA website at www.aicpa.org.